DREAMS
— *of* —
CHILDHOOD

Edited by Glorya Hale

LEOPARD

This edition published in 1995 by Leopard Books,
Random House, 20 Vauxhall Bridge Road, London SW1V 2SA

First published in the USA in 1994 by Gramercy Books

Designed by Melissa Ring

Printed and bound in China

ISBN 0 7529 0092 7

INTRODUCTION

For untold millennia, human beings have lived surrounded by some kind of visual imagery on whatever could be considered a wall. Historically, people have found these decorations reassuring, enlightening, entertaining, educational, or simply pleasing to the eye.

The earliest examples known are the wonderful cave paintings in Lascaux, in France. Highly stylized yet realistic animals cavort among tiny figures and even smaller handprints, which, perhaps, belonged to the children who watched while their mothers made the paintings to tell them of the world outside the cave. Although these cave paintings were done almost twenty thousand years ago, they are still vibrantly alive. No one really knows who painted them or why, but it is not too much to assume that part of their purpose was to decorate the walls of a dwelling—and enliven the life inside.

From the cave paintings at Lascaux, through the brightly colored Egyptian and Greco-Roman wall frescoes, to all the modes of wall decorating that followed, the same basic human impulse has been at work—the desire to live among pleasing visual images.

The principles of a successful display of images are maximum and most effective visibility, utilization of harmonies and contrasts, a balance of rest and movement for the eye, and an enlivening of the surroundings. All that's involved is learning a few simple techniques, and exercising your own creative imagination when you mat, frame, and hang the magnificent prints you'll find in this collection.

FRAMES FOR YOUR PICTURES

A frame should not be chosen in isolation from the picture, mat, and setting in which the finished print is to hang. Each of these elements influences the other and all should be considered together.

Finding or making precisely the right frame for a favorite old—or new, or unusual—picture is a simple pleasure, but a lasting one. It is, of course, possible to work with a professional framer and have the benefit of years of experience and expertise, but that is likely to be expensive, even if you assemble the elements at home. It is far more fun to spend some time leisurely browsing through antique shops and local flea markets, in a pleasant search for old frames, odd frames, frames that will be just right for your pictures. It is amazing what a bit of shrewd looking can turn up—old picture frames, frames from mirrors, interesting frames on appalling paintings. And you'll have the additional pleasure of recycling frames that may yet, either as they are or with a little care and attention, have a lifetime's use left in them. Old wood and tarnished brass can be stripped, stained, or polished to reveal hidden charm beneath the layers of paint and dirt.

Another possibility, and one with the potential for real joy,

is to learn an old, honored craft and make your own frames. There is no need to be an expert to achieve good, even beautiful, results. Imagine being surrounded by pieces of wood with elegant curves, the bracing smell of fresh sawdust, and a few simple tools. Imagine the deep satisfaction of creating something with your own hands that will permanently enhance not only your pictures but your home.

There are many books available that give easy-to-follow instructions for making frames. Or you could visit one of the stores that sell all the necessary materials and teach framemaking.

If you are interested in crafts, but have been hesitant about embarking on projects that seem too complex, involve learning too much at once, or entail too much initial expense, then framing could open a new world for you. It does not require a large initial outlay, a lot of space, or elaborate equipment. The first trials can be extremely simple, yet produce effective results. Then, as you acquire confidence, more subtle techniques and a bolder range of ideas can transform those first diffident steps into a lifelong adventure with a venerable yet always new craft.

DESIGNING A PICTURE WALL

There are no strict rules to be followed when designing a display of pictures. Each home is unique and reflects the occupants' tastes. What will give a picture wall its personality is your choice of subject matter, the colors of the mats, the style of framing you choose, and the panache of the arrangement. Some general guidelines and suggestions, however, may prove helpful.

First, take a good long look at the wall on which you want to arrange the pictures, and at the rest of the room in relation to that wall. Consider some practical details.

Are you dealing with a large, rectangular wall above a sofa? One dramatically framed picture or a carefully arranged group of pictures might be suitable. If you want to hang pictures on the wall of a long, narrow hallway, remember that there is no way to stand back from the pictures, so large images are probably inappropriate. A horizontal composition of smaller pictures, with interesting details that invite study at close range, might be the best solution.

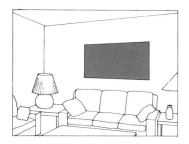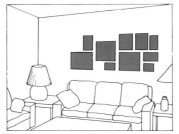

A high narrow space between two doors, on the other hand, might be most effectively filled with a vertical cluster of pictures with vertical emphases, or with one tall, narrow picture, its elongated quality accentuated by a mat wider at the top and bottom than at the sides.

The height at which a picture is hung affects its impact. The best position for a picture is at eye level. This will vary according to how the room is used. In a living room, for example, the picture wall should be comfortably visible when people are seated. Pictures hung above a sofa or chair must be sufficiently higher than the heads of those who will be seated there. The pictures in a child's room should be hung low enough for the child to enjoy them.

It is important to plan the total effect. After the holes have been made in the wall and the pictures have been hung, it is a little late to discover you have made a mistake. Spend some time beforehand designing the wall and experimenting with different arrangements.

A good method is to cut out pieces of stiff paper exactly the same shape and size as the framed prints and arrange them on the wall. They can be stuck on temporarily with masking tape and will give you a good idea of how the final arrangement will look. (The pieces of paper can be used later as templates

for marking off the position of the holes to be drilled for hooks or other hanging devices.) If possible, use paper of approximately the same overall color as the picture.

Some of the pictures may have strong compositional lines or color emphases. These can easily be indicated on the paper cutouts. Sketch directional lines in pencil or charcoal and indicate strong colors with colored paper or crayons. This will prevent having a display that works beautifully in terms of relative sizes and shapes from being ruined by an imbalance of color or by clashing directional lines.

Some people find it helpful to do an elevation drawing of the picture wall, particularly when a large arrangement is involved. These are not easy to do. Unless they are measured and drawn accurately, they can be misleading. The scale should be large enough for you to see what you are doing and small enough to be manageable. Try a scale of one inch to one foot (2.5 to 30 cm).

The elevation drawing—a nonperspective, vertical drawing of the wall—should also show doors, windows, and furniture. The positions of the pictures can be indicated in several ways.

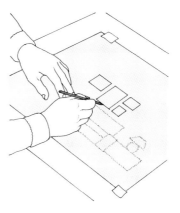

The pictures can be drawn in, also to scale, on the drawing or on a tracing-paper overlay carefully taped to the drawing. The overall sizes of the pictures can be changed by using larger or smaller mats and frames, so draw the pictures in the proportions you feel suit the arrangement. By using tracing-paper overlays, several arrangements can be recorded and the best ones chosen.

Another approach is to cut out small pieces of cardboard to represent the pictures and move them around on the drawing. This is a flexible working method. It is one of the best ways to learn about spacing and grouping pictures and to see how different shapes harmonize.

Cut the cardboard to the same scale as the elevation drawing, so the pieces represent the possible or actual picture sizes. For quick reference, mark the sizes on them and which picture each represents. Indicate strong colors or directional emphases. You might also want to cut cardboard to represent movable pieces of furniture.

Arranging Your Pictures

Reverie is a crucial part of creating an effective wall arrangement. Spend time looking, musing, imagining. Stare at the wall. This may well be the most fruitful part of the project. Try to imagine how you want the wall to look. The arrangement you imagine is the one to aim for. If you are careful and patient, you may achieve it.

After the initial stage of visualizing a display of pictures, the juggling begins, the struggle with the concrete elements of the composition—the images, mats, frames, and, of course, the intractable wall.

A large part of the joy in creating wall arrangements lies in the interplay of fancy and imagination with the materials you're working with and, in turn, with the simple realities of the room—the colors, the decor, the objects already present.

As with any other creative work, designing an arrangement of pictures—even if you are thinking only of how best to display a certain number of prints of one subject and period—will be a significant reflection of your personality.

Arranging a Group of Pictures

When you are arranging more than one picture on a wall, the challenge is to unify the group so the display can be seen as a whole rather than as a collection of unrelated pictures. There are no hard-and-fast rules, but there are some general guidelines that may be helpful.

Begin with the pictures themselves. Are they all the same size, shape, and subject, or are they all completely different? Are they all of the same period? Such factors are relevant to the arrangement you will eventually create.

Whatever the nature of the pictures and however they are to be arranged, the simplest, most basic way of unifying them is to align them in some way. This means that the top, bottom, or sides of each picture will line up with those of one or more of the others. This need not mean merely lining up the edges of the frames. Often other linear elements, like the mat

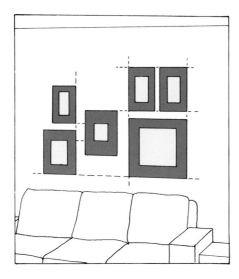

edges or even such directions as horizon lines in the composition of the pictures themselves, can be aligned in this way.

If you want a formal, symmetrical arrangement of images that are not all the same size and shape, they should be uniformly matted and framed, and all of them should be precisely aligned—tops, sides, and bottoms. Total symmetry, however, can be not only formal but boring, so it might be wise to break the alignment slightly with one larger or otherwise somewhat different picture.

The usual way to hang a group of pictures is to cluster them or to hang them in a line. A long horizontal line of pictures can be a good solution in a hallway or corridor, where the viewer will be standing or walking along. The pictures should be hung at eye level so they can be examined comfortably.

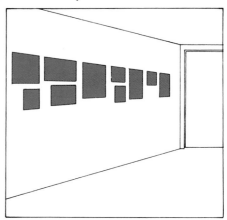

A vertical line of photographs often suits the space between two doors or between two tall pieces of furniture. To prevent monotony, occasionally break a horizontal or vertical line with a cluster of pictures or a larger one.

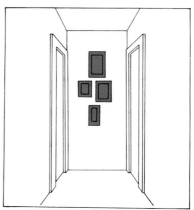

The arrangement of a cluster of pictures can be formal or informal. Formal arrangements are strictly symmetrical. An even number of pictures is placed on either side of an imaginary line, as if on a set of invisible scales. Pictures of the same visual weight balance each other. It is not necessary for all the images in the group to be the same size and shape. Use a mixture, as long as there is an even number of each size or shape so that one of each can be placed on either side of the "line." The formal feeling will be best sustained if the matching pictures have similar or even identical mats and frames.

Informal arrangements are usually asymmetrical. Each picture in the group can be different, since the point is to balance the general areas of the arrangement rather than the individual pictures. In other words, a group of small prints may balance one large one, or several tall, narrow prints may balance one rectangular one, but there are other variables in addition to this side-to-side juggling.

A good way to begin designing the arrangement, if the pictures are all different sizes, is to place the largest picture near the center of the arrangement and build out from it with the smaller pictures.

It can be helpful to think of the design as a tree with trunk and branches. The large picture is the trunk supporting the smaller prints which grow from it like branches and leaves. Like a real tree, the arrangement can grow into many different shapes—tall and narrow or broad and wide—controlled by the trunk, which is the center of balance.

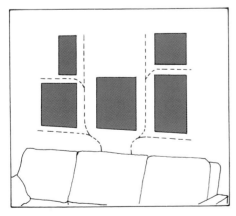

As the design grows, keep looking at the composition and checking to be sure it is neither top-heavy nor lopsided. Be sure that the overall shape remains pleasing and that pictures of the same size are distributed throughout and are not grouped together.

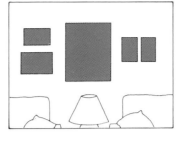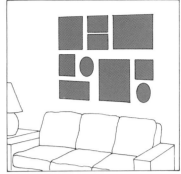

Take care neither to overcrowd the pictures nor to leave such wide spaces between them that they lose touch with each other and do not seem to be part of the same arrangement. As a general rule, the size of a picture determines the amount of space needed around it. Large images should usually be placed farther apart than small ones. Some open spaces of various sizes and shapes add interest and variety.

Displaying a Single Picture

You can create a dramatic focal point in a room with a single picture of the right size in the right space. It is even more important than with a group of images to balance the single picture with the surrounding decor. A cabinet, chair, or curtain near the picture will form an important part of the overall composition and should be carefully considered when you place the picture.

The size of the framed picture in relation to the size of the wall space is crucial. A small print will be lost on a large expanse of bare wall, but might be just right in a small, intimate corner, fitted between doors or pieces of furniture. A large picture should be hung where it will have the greatest impact. The room should be big enough that the viewer can stand back from the picture.

The shape of the wall space may require a particular picture shape. Of course, the shape of any picture can be changed with an appropriate mat and frame. Altering the proportions of the mat will affect the apparent shape of the print. A vertical picture, for example, can be made taller and thinner by widening the mat at the top and bottom, while a horizontal image will look wider if the top and bottom of the mat are narrower than the sides. An oval can be created by using a mat with an oval opening. Small pictures will look more impressive if they have large mats and frames.

A New View of Staircases

Picture arrangements on stairways pose unique problems and, therefore, unique challenges. These arrangements are seen from below, or from above, or from anywhere in between—while the observer is in motion. Any stair arrangement should, ideally, look good from each of these unusual perspectives. It should look as interesting when glanced at in passing as when it is contemplated more quietly.

An obvious solution would be to make an arrangement to go up, or down, in steps. But this is by no means the only solution. Others, less obvious, can be more satisfying. For these, the shape and size of the staircase, the position of the staircase in the room, and the points from which it is most likely to be viewed must be taken carefully into consideration. The more relaxed and playful the approach, the more likely is an intriguing and satisfying arrangement. Climbing stairs, too, can be an adventure.

A staircase has a different shape and function from the rest of the house, and the pictures hung in this area should be planned around its special characteristics.

Unlike wall arrangements in any other part of the house, those on either side of the steps have to be designed around the diagonal shape of the staircase. The diagonal design can be quite obvious, with groups of pictures placed parallel to the staircase. It can also be invisible. Even if the prints are hung in vertical or horizontal arrangements, the only pictures that will really be seen are those hung along the one diagonal line that corresponds to the eye level of the person ascending or descending.

The question of eye level, which is always a consideration when hanging pictures, is even more important when designing a staircase wall—unless the stairs are wide enough to make it possible to stand back from the arrangement. Those hung above and below the average eye level will probably not be seen often.

A spiral staircase is the exception. Since such a staircase usually stands in a corner or against a single wall, a vertically oriented picture arrangement is usually the only one possible.

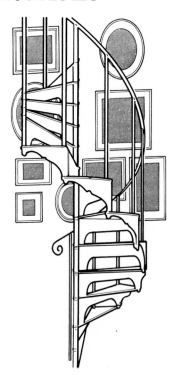

The landings of a staircase, of course, are like the rest of the house in terms of the design of wall arrangements. There is often a tall houseplant on a wide landing or a small table with a lamp or a vase of flowers. The display of pictures on the wall should be considered a design unit together with whatever else is on the landing, so that the whole ensemble forms a harmonious unit.

When hanging a picture on the wall at the top of the stairs, consider whether you prefer the whole image to be visible from the bottom of the stairs, or want it to reveal itself gradually on the way up.

If the staircase has been painted and carpeted in neutral tones, the pictures on the walls can determine the whole mood and color scheme. A staircase, unlike other areas in the house, which are full of furniture, curtains, and ornaments, has a minimum of decor to conflict with the images, so they can be the dominant factor. The pictures cannot, however, be chosen arbitrarily. The style and period feel of the pictures and the frames should either harmonize with or be in contrast to those of the staircase and, to a certain extent, to those of the rest of the house. But this remains a matter for personal taste and experimentation. There are no rules.

When designing a display of pictures for this area, remember that the whole staircase, including the landings and each flight of steps, should be treated as one wall arrangement. Nothing looks stranger than a sudden change of mood or theme halfway up a staircase.

The style of the framing and matting in the display will go a long way toward unifying the design. The same general style should be used throughout. The pictures could, for example, all be matted in the same color or all displayed in frames of the same period.

Preparing Your Pictures

Most of the prints in this book will fit into ready-made mats and frames. To those pictures that are irregular sizes—square, for example, or of a greater height in proportion to width—a light cream tone has been added as a border so that a ready-made mat and frame may be used. Should you prefer the picture without the border, you can trim it away and use a custom-made mat and frame. The background of some of the pictures can easily be trimmed so they will fit into smaller frames. Put the picture on a cutting board and, using a metal ruler and a No. 2 pencil, lightly mark the outer edges at the desired size. Use a craft knife and a metal ruler when cutting along the marked lines.

When choosing mats and frames, always take the pictures with you so you can select mats that enhance the pictures and also be certain that the openings in the mats are the correct size.

The pictures are perforated and easily removed. When removing a picture, it is best to put the book on a flat surface and pull the picture out with a slow but steady movement.

Mounting Pictures

Pictures used with standard-sized commercial mats and frames will not require mounting. You may, however, wish to increase the area around a picture with a larger mat and frame. Perhaps you have a lovely old frame that you would like to use, or you may want to display the picture on a wall where a larger, more dramatic presentation would be appropriate. Possibly you will want to use a custom-made square mat and frame. In these cases it is necessary to mount the picture so it fits the size frame required and stays in position when it is matted and framed.

A variety of mounting materials, including many types of cardboard, foam board, wood, and hardboard, are available. It's a good idea, therefore, to check an art supply shop for the mounting material best suited to the size of your picture and the manner in which you plan to display it. There are, however, a few general guidelines.

Often a print is mounted on a board that picks up one of the predominate colors. The picture can then be matted so a little of the mount shows. This approach may make it possible to fit an odd-sized picture into a standard-sized mat.

When a matted and framed picture will be less than twenty inches (50 cm) in height or width, it should be mounted on triple-weight mounting board. The mount should be cut slightly smaller than the channel of the frame so it will slide in easily.

When a matted and framed picture will be more than twenty inches (50 cm) in height or width, a stiffer mounting material, such as hardboard, should be used.

For an extremely light frame, light—but strong—plastic foam mounting board is a good choice.

The simplest way to mount a picture at home is to glue it to the mounting board. Most of the adhesives made for home use are suitable for mounting. Rubber cement, however, should be avoided because it tends to lose its adhesive properties when it dries.

There are several spray adhesives on the market. These are easy to use and effective, as long as the manufacturer's instructions are followed exactly. Some types dry instantly, others more slowly, allowing time to reposition the picture. The first spray from the can often results in a heavy application of adhesive that will subsequently seep out from under

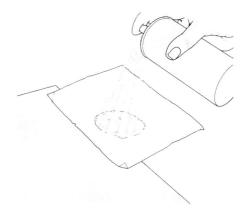

the edges of the picture, so it is advisable to begin spraying to one side of the picture on a piece of scrap paper.

Tape is easy to use for mounting, but it may disintegrate in time. Double-sided tape can be used, but once put down with the tape a picture cannot be repositioned. So unless you are perfectly confident, don't try to use it.

ALL ABOUT MATTING

A mat creates a link between the picture, the frame, and the decor of the room in which the picture is hung. It also protects the picture. Consequently, a mat is one of the most important elements in the framing process. Great care is required in choosing the right color, material, and width of the mat when buying it or having it made, and precision is essential when measuring and cutting it yourself.

Even the simplest picture can be transformed by surrounding it with a simple mat. When the mat is well proportioned, the picture will immediately have depth and distinction. But a simple, conventionally proportioned mat, although undeniably attractive, is the least of what can be done once you consider the potential of mats.

A mat is the setting for a picture and will strongly affect its tone, style, and mood. The elements to consider are the size, shape, and proportion of the mat in relation to the texture and color of the matting material. Such accents as fine ink lines drawn close to the picture, or a bit of the mount showing, can add definition or create the illusion of a double mat. Sometimes a double, or even a triple, mat can be strikingly effective, but it must be cut with extreme care, since the inner mat is usually much narrower than the outer one and the two edges are very close together. Commercial double mats are available, but they are difficult to find in every size and color. It is relatively inexpensive, however, to have a mat custommade in a framing shop.

You may never realize the potential of your pictures until you begin to experiment with matting them. A simple image can suddenly leap into life when the basically circular shape of the composition is emphasized by a mat's circular opening. Or a Victorian die cut may be highlighted by an oval in a mat of antiqued parchment. A picture often gains luminosity and depth when surrounded by a mat that picks up one of its dominant colors. And there is always the intriguing possibility of assembling a group of small pictures, and unifying them into an integrated composition within an appropriately colored and textured multiple mat.

Like frames, mats can be bought or found or made. Since mats are usually made of cardboard, and the only necessary tools are a metal straightedge and a sharp craft knife, making mats is a simple and satisfying way to begin exploring your potential framing skills. After the initial discovery that you can cut a straight line with precision, there is a lot of experimentation to be done. You can play with the design effects of covered mats, perhaps, or try double mats in contrasting colors and textures. Old photograph albums, found in almost any flea market, and fairly inexpensive, can be a good source of mats.

Matting Materials

The thin cardboard used for mats is available in a wide range of colors and textures. Mat board covered with gold foil, cork, and fabric is also available, but can be difficult to cut. It is often easier to buy a cardboard mat and cut it to size, then cover it with the desired material. When choosing a matting material, it is important that the color and texture enhance the picture, rather than overwhelm it.

Equipment

The equipment needed for cutting a mat is simple but should be of good quality. It includes a very sharp craft knife, a metal ruler, a large square or set square, a cutting board, and a sharp pencil.

Cutting paper blunts the edges of blades quickly, so a knife must be sharpened frequently or the blade changed often.

A special cutting tool for mats is available that makes cutting a beveled edge particularly easy, although a sharp craft knife and straightedge work well.

Measuring the Mat

First cut the outer edges of the mat to fit into the frame you will use. The mat should be slightly smaller than the frame so it will easily slide into the channel. Check the outer dimensions of the mat and be sure it is square. If it is irregular, the opening cannot be measured or cut accurately and the whole mat will be distorted.

Check the right angles at the corners of the board with the square or straightedge. They should be exactly 90 degrees.

To trim an irregular mat, place the straightedge along the side of the board and draw a pencil line on the board to give an absolutely straight line from which to work.

Place the large set square against the straightedge and draw a line at right angles to the first line.

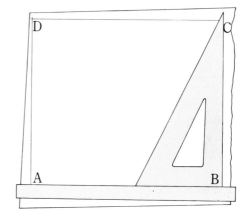

Measure the line AB. Place the square on B and draw a line BC, at the right angles to AB. AD and BC can now be measured and the points DC connected.

When trimmed along these lines, the mat will be absolutely square and ready for the opening to be cut.

Cutting the Opening

After the mat board has been cut, checked, and, if necessary, trimmed, use a metal ruler to mark the position of the opening. The opening should overlap the picture by about one-eighth of an inch (3 mm) all around. The pictures in this book are approximately one-eighth of a inch (3 mm) larger than the opening in the appropriate commercial mat, to allow for slight variations in the mat.

The opening can be drawn in lightly with pencil, or the corners can be marked with tiny pinholes. If pencil is used, it is best to draw the lines on the back of the mat board and to cut the board on that side so no marks will show on the front surface.

The edges of the opening can be cut either vertically or beveled. A vertical edge is less obtrusive and is often used for double or triple mats. It tends, however, to cast shadows. The beveled edge, on the other hand, makes the mat look more finished, casts no shadow on the picture, and gives a greater feeling of depth to the picture.

To avoid ruining matting board and to get accustomed to the tools, it is a good idea to practice cutting on scrap pieces of cardboard before cutting the mat itself. Cutting the corners in particular may take time to master.

Lay the blade of the craft knife against either the 90-degree or the 45-degree edge of the straightedge, depending on the cut required. Cut as smoothly as possible, at a steady pace, from corner to corner. Do not stop in the middle of a side or slow down at the corners because this may change the appearance of the cut. Be careful, too, not to overcut the corners. The tip of the blade should just penetrate the mat board.

Keep a steady pressure on the knife at all times, and be careful to keep the angle at which you are cutting consistent. Pretend your wrist is rigid.

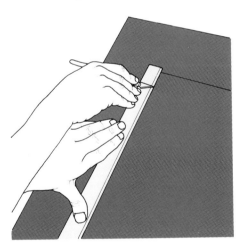

When all four sides have been cut, the center piece of cardboard should lift out easily. A sharp razor blade can be used for neatening the corners, and fine sandpaper or a fine emery board will smooth the edges of the cut.

Double and Triple Mats

A single opening with the edges of two, or even three, mats showing can create an interesting effect. The opening in the upper mat is cut slightly wider to reveal a narrow strip, called a fillet, of the lower mat around the picture. Three mats can be used in the same way to make a triple opening. The fillet focuses attention on the picture by outlining it against the

mat. It can be darker or lighter than the mat, or can pick out one of the colors in the picture or in the surrounding room.

When the edges of the openings are beveled, showing two or three thin white lines, the effect can be striking.

When making a double mat, instead of using mat board for the narrow inner mat, try a piece of heavy colored paper, left unbeveled. The light border added to some of the pictures in this book can serve as a fillet.

To avoid monotony, it is important with double and triple mats to make the fillets, frame, and mat all different widths.

Instead of cutting the openings before fastening the mats together, it may be easiest to cut the largest opening first. Then attach the two mats together with double-sided tape and cut the second opening through the first. If a third mat is to be used, attach it next and cut through the other openings.

Multiple Matting

Multiple matting is a simple and economical way to create a variety of arrangements. The term means that several openings are cut in the same mat. The arrangement is then treated as a whole, covered with a single piece of glass, and hung as if it were one image. There is great flexibility; the pictures can be brought together because of their subject matter, color values, or even because they just look good together. The principle of selection is only that the pictures come together in some kind of coherent group and are enhanced by each other's presence.

After you have selected the pictures you want to use in a multiple display, choose a mat color that will enhance all of them. It is usually best to stay in a fairly neutral range and use a black, white, or creamy beige mat, although if there is a dominant or common color in the pictures a mat that matches it or contrasts effectively can be used.

Group the pictures on the mounting board to decide on the right arrangement and spacing. Pay particular attention to the way the compositional lines of the individual pictures relate to each other and try each picture in several different positions. Experiment with the spacing. A good rule is to make the border around the assembly wider than the spaces between the individual pictures.

Decide on the size and shape of the final assembly in relation to the format of the pictures. A row of vertical pictures, for example, might look most dramatic in a long, horizontal frame. For a large assembly, it may not be possible to buy mat board of the required size. In this case, two pieces of mat board can be butted together and covered with fabric, or hardboard that is one-eighth of an inch (3 mm) thick can be used instead.

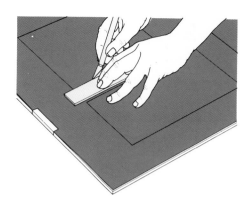

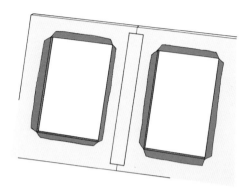

When the pictures have been arranged, check to be sure that the vertical spaces between them are equal, even if the horizontal spaces are irregular. Do this first by eye, then check the space with a ruler.

When the spacing is satisfactory, mark the mounting board clearly at the corners of each print. These marks will not show after the mat is put on. Glue the pictures to the mounting board, starting at one end of the assembly and working across.

With masking tape, attach a piece of tracing paper the same size as the mat to the top of the mounting board, covering the prints and the board. With a straightedge and pencil trace the pictures, making the tracing one-sixteenth of an inch (1.6 mm) smaller on all sides than the prints. Remove the tracing paper and tape it to the mat board, making sure it is absolutely square.

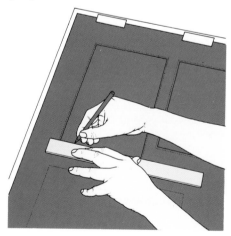

With a sharp craft knife and a straightedge, cut out the openings in the mat, cutting through both tracing paper and board. It is easiest to cut all the vertical lines first, then all the horizontal lines.

After the openings have been cut, remove the tracing paper, turn the mat over, and apply adhesive to the back.

Lower the mat carefully over the mounting board, lining up the openings with the prints. Cover with a piece of cardboard and weights, such as heavy books.

After the adhesive has dried, it may be necessary to trim the mat and mounting board.

As a final touch to unify the assembly, a thin black line can be ruled around the outside of each print with a fine-pointed black pen.

Covering a Mat with Fabric

Sometimes a picture seems to demand a fabric mat. An elegant floral print, for example, might seem best set off by a mat of natural linen or silk. Pictures for a little girl's room can be charming matted in a cotton with a small print.

For the mat board that is to be covered, choose a color close to but not darker than the fabric.

Measure and cut the mat. Cut a piece of fabric at least one inch (2.50 cm) larger than the outside dimensions of the mat.

Spread an appropriate adhesive evenly on the front of the mat.

Press the adhesive-covered surface to the back of the fabric.

Turn the mat over and press the fabric onto the mat with your hands until it is smooth.

Turn the mat over again, and using a sharp craft knife, carefully trim the fabric along the edge of the mat.

Then make a cut in the fabric diagonally out from each corner. Cut out the center opening leaving one inch (2.5 cm) extra along the inner edge.

Apply adhesive along the inner edge of the back of the mat. Pull the fabric around the inner edge and press it into the adhesive on the mat.

PUTTING EVERYTHING TOGETHER

After the picture has been mounted and the mat and the frame have been made, all that remains is to put all the elements together, then add glass and the backing board.

Glazing

Glass protects the picture and will also enhance its appearance. Colors have greater richness under glass. Glass also creates the illusion of greater space, since it reflects some of the color and light of the surrounding room. The only disadvantage to glazing a photograph is that it makes the picture heavier and more fragile, and when a frame is not properly sealed, condensation can form behind the glass.

For glazing, picture glass is usually used. Picture glass is only about one-sixteenth of an inch (1.6 mm) thick and free of the flaws sometimes found in window glass.

Most ready-made frames, available in art supply stores, come with glass and a backing board. If you require glass for a frame, however, a framing or hardware shop will cut it to measure for you.

Backing the Picture

A sheet of double-faced corrugated cardboard placed behind the picture will add stiffening. It will also protect the picture from possible knocks or falls. Sometimes an extra sheet or two of cardboard must be used so that the elements fit snugly in the channel of the frame.

Assembling the Picture

Before putting all the elements together, be sure that they are clean. Check that the channel is smooth and that there is no dried glue to prevent the glass from fitting neatly. Gently clean any stains or fingerprints from the mat with an eraser. (Remember to test the eraser on a scrap of mat board first.) Clean the glass thoroughly.

Lay the frame facedown. Carefully put in the glass, followed by the mat, the picture, and the backing board. Press lightly, but do not try to expel all the air. Some room is necessary to permit the cardboard to contract and expand in response to environmental changes in temperature and humidity.

Most ready-made frames come with clips to close the framed picture. If your frame does not come with clips, use brads. Press a small brad (it should be five-eighths of an inch—1.5 cm) about halfway down each vertical inside edge of the molding. Pliers, a special brad pusher, or a tack hammer can be used to do this. If pliers are used, insert some padding between the pliers and the outside edge of the molding to protect the frame. If you are using a hammer, you can clamp the frame, protected by a block of wood, to the work surface to hold it steady while you tap the nails in.

Inspect the frame, and if everything is correctly positioned, insert the other brads about four inches (10 cm) apart, working from the center of each side toward the corners.

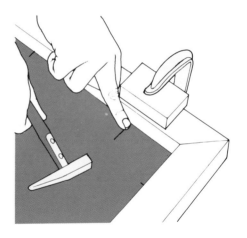

Hanging Your Pictures

Many types of hardware are available for hanging your pictures. Some are invisible, others ornamental; some are specially designed for light or for heavy pictures and some for different wall surfaces.

The devices most widely used on the backs of framed pictures are screw eyes, D-rings, and sawtooth hangers. Magnetic tape can be used to hang pictures on metal, and Velcro is excellent for hanging lightweight pictures.

Screw eyes and D-rings are attached to both of the vertical sides of the frame, about one-third down from the top, and as close to the inside edge as possible. It is advisable to use an awl or a push drill to make a pilot hole before screwing in the eye. Picture wire is then threaded through the eyes, taut enough so that it does not show above the frame. The ends of the wire should be wound tightly and close to the eye. The wire can then be hung on a picture hanger that has been hammered into the wall.

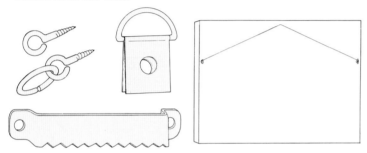

Although screw eyes and picture wire constitute one of the simplest and most traditional methods of hanging a framed picture, there are several disadvantages. The picture tends to slip out of alignment easily, and often the top of the frame tips forward from the wall. These problems can be solved by using two hooks on the wall instead of one and by placing the screw eyes as near to the top of the frame as possible.

Sawtooth metal hangers, which have pointed notches that hook on a nail in the wall, will keep the framed picture flat against the wall and prevent it from shifting out of alignment. One type of hanger has square indentations, as well as the sawtooth notches, and can be used with picture hangers. The hangers are fastened to the top corners of the frame, with one screw fastened to the vertical side, so that weight is evenly distributed. For heavier pictures, screws set in plugs in the wall, and not screwed in fully, can be used instead of picture hangers.

Magnetic tape makes it possible to hang pictures on partitions and other surfaces that are metal. Simply put the tape on the back of the picture, then press it against the wall. Since it adheres quite strongly, the tape should only be put around the edges of the picture.

Velcro fabric fasteners make a secure hanging device for lightweight pictures. When the two strips of material are pressed together, they grip tenaciously. With one strip well glued to the wall and the other to the picture, the Velcro can support a fairly substantial weight.

Sometimes the decor of a room, the picture itself, or the ornateness of the frame seems to demand that an ornamental hanging device be used. Decorative rings that screw into the frame are available. Some pictures are enhanced when hung with brass chains or elegant velvet cord from decorative hooks. Pictures in small, light frames can be attached to ribbons and hung in strips.

A variety of wall attachments are available for different kinds of walls and for pictures of varying weights:

The picture hanger is the simplest, easiest, and most common device to use. This small metal hook is paired with a slim masonry nail that leaves only a tiny hole in the wall, yet can support a fairly heavy picture. It is quite adequate for most inside walls.

Toggle bolts, which have a folding claw that passes through a hole and, when tightened, opens out to grip the back of the panel, are excellent for thin paneled walls.

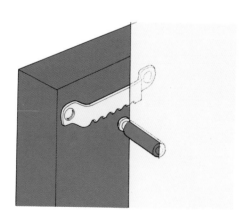

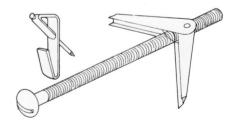

A plug inserted into the wall for a nail or wood screw is best for masonry and brick walls. There are a number of plugs available, including expanding ones made of metal or plastic. They come with full instructions.

THE PICTURES

M.E.GRAY.

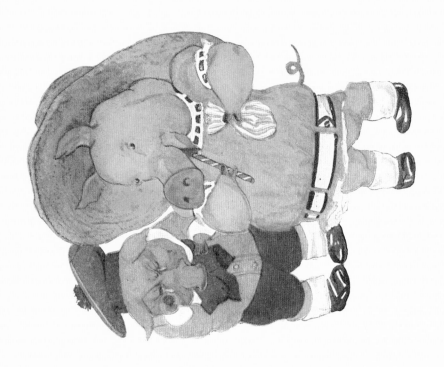